Money Mastery for Millennials: The No-Nonsense Guide to Managing Your Money in Your 20s

Money Mastery for Millennials: The No-Nonsense Guide to Managing Your Money in Your 20s

Copyright © 2024 by **Esther Bukar**

Table of Content

Introduction

Money: a ubiquitous aspect of our lives--one that elicits complex emotions and behaviors. In youth, we often grapple with its scarcity; however, as we mature—our relationship to it evolves. As we grow older, we strive for financial stability and independence.

More than ever, millennials must master the art of wise financial management. Their formative years coincided with a colossal economic recession, setting them apart from preceding generations. The burden we bear in terms of astronomical student loan debt upon graduation is unprecedented. Jobs were scarce, incomes stagnant, and the housing market had crumbled.

The perplexity that often engulfs millennials regarding their finances shouldn't be a surprise: the majority of us never received formal education in budgeting, saving, or investing during our formative years. Regrettably—despite being indispensable life skills—these crucial money management techniques eluded both school curriculum and parental guidance. So we've had to wing it.

Living paycheck to paycheck or accumulating credit card debt exacerbates your financial stresses. Empower yourself with financial education as knowledge equips you powerfully for money management. That's where this book comes in.

Why Financial Literacy Matters

Financial literacy entails a comprehensive understanding of fundamental money management principles: budgeting; emergency savings allocation–a critical component for handling unforeseen circumstances, debts clearance and credit building activities are also key facets. Furthermore--investing in future prospects stands as an integral part in this multifaceted concept.

Mastering the core money skills can indeed revolutionize your financial life: you will consistently pay bills on time; accumulate savings for unforeseen expenses, and harness the power of investment to maximize earnings. Financial literacy empowers you--it ensures that you control your money, rather than being controlled by it.

Millennials, with decades of potential earning ahead, can significantly improve their long-term financial standing by cultivating early literacy in this field. The financial decisions one makes during their 20s are pivotal: they lay the groundwork not only for subsequent years but also extend and influence into future decades such as those in your 30s, 40s--and beyond.

Start saving and investing now: your money will undergo years of growth and compounding. The impact of an additional decade--a period characterized by compound growth on your investments--is indeed enormous.

Financial mistakes made early in life, meanwhile, may incur significant costs: poor credit and accrued debt during one's twenties can impede future loan acquisitions - notably a mortgage. Consequently, the dream of home ownership slides further from grasp; indeed it seems almost elusive. Retirement savings also take a hit, making your golden years less comfortable.

Armed with financial acumen, millennials have the capacity to dodge these expensive missteps and forge a secure future. As you educate yourself in this moment, you set your finances on an advantageous trajectory.

Overview of Key Money Management Principles

To put it simply: successful money management fundamentally hinges on one principle--spending less than what you earn. The question, however, remains; how can this be translated into actionable practice?

The book offers bespoke answers to the financial scenarios unique to millennials. It delves into an overview of fundamental money mastery, covering:

Design a pragmatic budget that harmonizes with your income, financial objectives, and lifestyle to exercise control over your finances. Balancing saving with expenditure becomes more manageable through effective budgeting. Applications amplify the ease of adhering to a budget in unprecedented ways.

Debt Reduction: Strategizing to Swiftly Pay Down Credit Card Balances, Student Loans, and Other Financial Liabilities. Engage in these strategies to promptly pay down your credit card balances, student loans and other debts that burden you financially; through this proactive approach--you can minimize interest payments and unshackle yourself from the relentless grip of debt.

Master the art of constructing an "Emergency Savings," a proverbial rainy-day fund equivalent to three to six months' worth of your living expenses; this will serve as your safety net for unanticipated bills or instances where income is lost.

Harness the power of compound interest in your retirement savings by initiating investments during your 20s; seize full advantage of workplace retirement plans, particularly 401(k) accounts.

Should you rent or buy housing? Learn the strategies for saving towards a downpayment and comprehending mortgage options. Additionally, grasp the tactics of wealth accumulation through real estate.

Side hustles: These are part-time gigs and side businesses-- ideas that generate extra income. You can utilize this surplus to accelerate your savings or pay off debt more rapidly; it's a flexible financial booster for you.

Investing Basics: These are simple, beginner-level strategies that can propel your money into higher returns over an extended period; they form the foundation of any investment plan.

Ways to cultivate good money habits on a modest income include: spending less; saving aggressively; living below your means, and delaying gratification.

The book dispels the myth necessitating wealth for financial advancement; indeed, with a strategic approach, even individuals earning average salaries can incrementally increase their net worth.

Book Roadmap

Organized into seven chapters, *Money Mastery for Millennials* focuses on specific aspects of personal finance that are critical for young adults.

Each chapter in this book employs a carefully crafted structure that progressively guides you towards mastering wealth. Throughout your journey, expect to encounter not only actionable tips but also practical examples and real-world advice on effectively executing the outlined strategies.

This book distills the core principles of financial literacy, providing millennials with a robust financial education and empowering them to prosper economically. The topics covered span a wide range; however, our focus remains steadfast on equipping millennials with actionable knowledge for thriving financially.

A bullet point summary of the key takeaways concludes each chapter, allowing you to conveniently reference the book as a cheat sheet later for reinforcing financial lessons and habits.

This book empowers millennials with the clarity, confidence and skills necessary to master their finances. They can bid farewell to money worries; instead, they will stride confidently into a future where smart financial decisions become second nature at every turn.

Let's begin: the earlier you initiate the process of enhancing your financial knowledge, a more promising future awaits.

Chapter 1: Developing a Millionaire Mindset

Many people dream of becoming millionaires. But most never get there. Why is that? It's not just about having the right financial strategies and habits. Your mindset and beliefs about money also play a huge role in building wealth.

The way you think about and approach money matters. In this chapter, you'll learn how to adopt an empowering millionaire mindset so you can crush your financial goals.

Adopting Positive Beliefs About Money

Your core beliefs influence how you behave with money. If you view money negatively, you'll have a hard time accumulating it. Your behaviors and actions will reflect those negative beliefs.

For example, if you believe:

- Money is the root of all evil

- Rich people are greedy

- I'll never be wealthy

Then it becomes a self-fulfilling prophecy. Your actions align with your beliefs, sabotaging your ability to get ahead financially.

To become a money master, you need to eliminate limiting beliefs like these. Instead, adopt empowering beliefs about money, such as:

- Money allows me to live the lifestyle I want

- Money gives me freedom and control over my life

- I deserve to be financially successful

- My income is determined by the value I provide to others

- Investing allows my money to grow

Write down any negative money beliefs you have. Then write down positive affirmations to replace them. Say these new affirmations aloud daily. Over time, they will override the old beliefs.

Surround yourself with people who have succeeded financially. Their positive outlook will rub off on you. Read books and listen to podcasts by money masters. Feed your mind with their uplifting stories and wisdom.

Tip: Follow entrepreneurs, investors, and finance experts on social media. Observe how they think, talk, and approach money. Model their mindset.

Delayed Gratification and Goal Setting

Americans live in a culture of instant gratification. With one-click shopping and fast food, we expect to get what we want, when we want.

But this impulse for immediate pleasure keeps many people broke. Buying everything you want right now means less money for the future.

To build wealth, you need self-discipline. You must delay immediate gratification for greater rewards later. For example:

- Pack a lunch instead of eating out daily

- Hold back on splurging on the latest iPhone or game console

- Keep driving your used car instead of upgrading to a brand new one

- Save diligently before taking a dream trip

Making small sacrifices adds up. That money can be invested to grow your net worth exponentially over decades.

Get comfortable being uncomfortable. Understand that real success takes patience and deferred gratification. Trust that your future self will thank you.

Goal setting goes hand in hand with delayed gratification. Clearly define your short and long-term money goals. Give each goal a specific price tag and timeline. For example:

Short-term goals:

- Save $2,000 for an emergency fund in 6 months

- Pay off $5,000 in credit card debt in 1 year

Long-term goals:

- Save $50,000 for a house downpayment in 5 years

- Accumulate $1 million in investment assets by age 50.

Write your goals down and revisit them often to stay motivated. Share goals related to debt payoff, saving for a house, etc with a friend to keep each other accountable.

Celebrate when you hit a milestone, then set your next goal. The reward of achieving financial targets will keep you fired up to delay gratification again and again.

Overcoming Limiting Thoughts and Scarcity Mentality

Fear and limiting beliefs about money often stem from scarcity mentality. This is the feeling that you'll never have enough money, so you have to cling tightly to every dollar.

Scarcity mentality causes:

- Excessive penny pinching

- Unwillingness to spend on necessities

- Fear of investing and losing money

- Constant money anxiety and worry

Here are antidotes to scarcity thinking:

Remember money is a renewable resource. The world is not running out of money. There are endless opportunities to make more.

Focus on increasing your income streams. Earning more allows greater saving and investing. Update your skills. Change jobs or negotiate a raise to boost your cash inflows.

Celebrate money wins. Instead of just focusing on what you don't have, celebrate money milestones. Your first $1,000 saved. Paying off a student loan. Reaching a net worth target. Celebrate abundance.

Find your enough number. Determine how much money you need to be content. Realize you don't need millions to feel financially secure.security.

Give to others. Donating money or time actually increases feelings of prosperity. You realize how much you have to give.

Invest for the long run. Understand that market downturns are temporary while the overall trend is upwards. Reinvest dividends and gains. Think decades, not days.

Educate yourself. Learn investing basics so you're not paralyzed by fear of losing money. Knowledge replaces money worries with confidence.

Visualize success. Imagine the life experiences and sense of freedom that financial success will bring. This inspires positive money behaviors.

Surround yourself with abundance. Follow entrepreneurs and investors on social media. Read books on wealth creation. Immerse yourself in an environment of prosperity thinking.

These tips will help you cultivate an abundant money mindset. You'll overcome scarcity fears holding you back from achieving your financial goals.

The path to wealth begins in your mind. Adopt empowering money beliefs that will drive your behaviors and habits. See money as a tool for good, not evil. Know you deserve financial success. Delay immediate gratification today for a more prosperous tomorrow.

Chapter 1 Summary

- Examine your core beliefs and assumptions about money. Do they empower you or hold you back?

- Replace negative money beliefs with positive affirmations. Repeat daily.

- Delay gratification and save today to build wealth for your future self.

- Set short and long-term financial goals with specific dollar amounts.

- Celebrate money milestones. Focus on abundance, not scarcity.

- Invest for the long run. Education conquers fear.

- Visualize your ideal life enabled by financial success.

Chapter 2: Budgeting Basics

Budgeting. For many, this word evokes frustration or boredom. But having a budget is the foundation for financial success. A budget aligns your spending with your values and goals. It prevents you from mindlessly frittering away your paycheck.

In this chapter, you'll learn budgeting basics. We'll cover how to create a realistic budget tailored to your lifestyle. You'll learn how to prioritize needs versus wants. And tips to help you stick to your budget so you can achieve your financial goals.

How to Create a Realistic Budget

First, tally up all of your monthly income after taxes. This includes your salary, freelance work, investment income, contributions from a partner, etc. Be realistic about estimating side income.

Next, total up your fixed monthly expenses. These are predictable costs like:

- Rent

- Car payment

- Insurance premiums

- Minimum debt payments

- Utility bills

- Subscriptions

Then estimate variable expenses that fluctuate like:

- Groceries

- Dining out

- Entertainment

- Clothes and personal items

- Gas and transportation

Use a budgeting app or spreadsheet to add up all of your income and expenses. If your expenses exceed your income, you'll need to trim discretionary spending.

Build your budget around your financial priorities like saving for an emergency fund or paying off high interest debt quickly.

Allow some room in your budget for fun. Deprivation leads to binge spending. Allocate a "blow money" category you can spend guilt-free.

Once you've created a balanced budget, commit to sticking to it for at least 3 months. Adjust as needed after tracking your actual spending.

Prioritizing Needs vs Wants

Budgeting is about aligning expenses with your values and goals, not denying yourself. But you'll need to ruthlessly cut discretionary spending that adds little to your life.

The 50/30/20 budget rule is an easy guideline to follow:

- 50% of income covers needs like housing and bills

- 30% goes to wants like hobbies, dining out, vacations

- 20% goes to savings and debt repayment

Distinguish between things you truly want, and fleeting desires. Fulfilling a temporary desire won't make you happier long-term.

For example, dining out because you enjoy it is a want. Buying a flashy car to impress others is a fleeting desire. Go for substance over status symbols.

Follow the "one in, one out rule." Only buy something new after selling or returning something you already own. This prevents clutter from accumulating.

Delay big purchases that aren't urgent. Wait a few weeks or months before making a final decision. Time often cures impulsive spending urges.

Tips for Sticking to Your Budget

Making a budget is simple. But actually sticking to it is the hard part. Here are tips to make budgeting a habit:

- **Make budgeting a game.** See how low you can get certain spending categories each month. Challenge yourself to spend less than last month.

- **Automate saving and bill payments** so the money leaves your account before you can spend it.

- **Track spending diligently.** This creates accountability and awareness around where your money goes.

- **Avoid temptations.** Unsubscribe from retail email lists. Hide your credit cards so they aren't top of wallet.

- **Find a budget buddy.** Share your budget with a friend. Check in regularly and celebrate sticking to your goals.

- **Use cash for discretionary spending.** The physical act of handing over cash makes you more mindful about purchases.

- **Plan affordable social outings.**Suggest potlucks or going hiking with friends instead of happy hour.

- **Give yourself a buffer.** Your budget estimates will never be 100% accurate. Allocate extra savings as a buffer for surprises.

- **Let go of budget shaming.** Don't beat yourself for slip-ups. Gently get back on track without dwelling on the past.

- **Make budgeting a habit.** After 2-3 months of diligence, budgeting will feel automatic. You may even grow to like restricting spending!

Apps and Tools to Automate Saving

Technology can make budgeting effortless. Here are some of the most popular money apps:

Mint – Link all your accounts. Mint automatically categorizes spending and creates budgets based on your historical spending data.

Personal Capital – Provides net worth and cash flow tracking. Monitors all your accounts in one dashboard. Has robust investment analysis tools.

Digit – Analyzes your income and spending patterns. Automatically transfers "excess" money into savings based on what you can afford.

Acorns – Rounds up everyday purchases and invests the spare change. Makes passive investing and saving easy.

You Need a Budget (YNAB) – User-friendly budgeting software helps you allocate every dollar so you don't overspend. Has mobile app.

EveryDollar – Dave Ramsey's budgeting app focuses on giving every dollar a purpose through zero-based budgeting philosophy.

Pick one budgeting app to use consistently. The automation will save you time while helping you spend mindfully and save more.

Chapter 2 Summary

- Add up monthly income and fixed and variable expenses to create a budget.

- Distinguish between needs, wants, and fleeting desires when making spending decisions.

- Implement strategies like budget gamification and automation to make sticking to a budget easier.

- Use budgeting apps and tools to track spending and automate saving.

- Give yourself a buffer since budget estimates will never be perfect.

- Make budgeting a habit through consistency over 2-3 months.

Chapter 3: Managing Debt

Debt has become normalized in our society. Terms like "good debt" and "leverage" make borrowing sound appealing. But the truth is, debt holds many millennials back financially.

In this chapter, you'll learn how to manage debts wisely. We'll cover which debts to aggressively pay off versus which loans can accelerate wealth when used strategically. You'll also get tips for reducing credit card debt, student loans, and improving your credit.

Understanding Good Debt vs Bad Debt

Not all debts are created equal. Bad debt has high interest rates and no long-term payoff. Good debt helps you earn more than the cost of borrowing.

Bad debts examples:

- Credit cards - Average interest rate of 16% or higher. No asset building.

- Payday loans - Extremely high interest loans that trap borrowers in cycles of debt.

- Luxury cars - Rapid depreciation plus interest makes them a poor investment.

Pay off bad debt immediately using the "debt snowball" method. List debts smallest to largest. Pay minimums on all debts except the smallest. Attack the smallest debt with a vengeance until paid off. Repeat with the next smallest debt.

As you pay off debts, your available cash flow snowballs. This builds momentum to knock out debts faster.

Good debt examples:

- Mortgages - Interest rates around 3-5%. Allows you to own an appreciating asset (real estate).

- Student loans - Enables education and skills to earn higher income long-term.

- Business loans - Funds growth opportunities that increase profits greater than loan costs.

Use good debt strategically. For example, deduct mortgage interest from your taxes. Make minimum student loan payments while investing excess cash into retirement accounts.

Focus on raising your income aggressively so you can pay off bad debt and maximize good debt faster.

Strategies for Paying Off Student Loans

If you have student loan debt, here are strategies to pay it off faster:

Make extra principal payments. Paying even $20-50 extra per month directly reduces your principal balance, saving money on interest.

Target high interest loans first. If you have multiple loans at different rates, focus on the highest interest loans to save the most.

Refinance or consolidate loans. You may qualify for lower interest rates, getting you closer to paying off debt faster. Shop around for the best terms.

Change repayment plans. Income-based plans cap payments at a percentage of your income. While balances grow in the short run, the smaller payment helps you stay on track.

Find employer repayment assistance. Ask if your company offers student loan repayment benefits. $100 per month in repayment assistance adds up.

Take a payment vacation. Federal loans allow you to temporarily pause payments if facing financial hardship. Use the paused payments to pay down credit cards or save up cash.

Dedicate raises and bonuses. Allocate extra influxes of cash directly towards debt repayment. Celebrate by visualizing the declining loan balance.

Side hustle. Generate extra income from a part-time job or freelancing that goes straight to debt repayment.

Paying off student loans requires consistency and sacrifice upfront. But debt freedom is well worth delaying gratification today.

Credit Card Debt Reduction Tips

The average credit card interest rate is over 16%. That's highway robbery! But there are ways to outsmart credit card companies so you can pay off balances faster:

Consolidate with a 0% balance transfer card. Transfer all your credit card balances onto a new card offering 0% interest for 12-18 months. Use the intro period to pay off debt aggressively without accruing interest.

Only make minimum payments on all but the smallest card. With the debt snowball method, attack the smallest balance first while paying minimums on the other cards. As you pay off cards, roll the payments to the next card.

Cut up excess cards. Don't cancel cards as that hurts your credit. But do cut up little used cards and stick to one primary card to limit spending temptation.

Ask for a lower interest rate. Simply calling your credit card company and asking nicely for a lower rate often works surprisingly well. Be ready to politely threaten taking your business elsewhere.

Pay more than the minimum. Minimum payments are designed to keep you in debt for life. Pay double or triple the minimum whenever possible.

Pay before the due date. Pay your bill as soon as the charge clears, not by the due date. Less time accruing interest saves you money.

Avoid cash advances. These incur astronomical interest rates immediately, unlike purchases which have a grace period. Never acceptable.

Stop using cards until balances are paid. Commit to not using credit cards to buy anything new until existing balances are paid in full. Break the debt cycle.

With consistency, you can pay off five-figure credit card debt in under 3 years. Cut up cards, consolidate, pay early and often. You've got this!

Improving Your Credit Score in Your 20s

Your credit score determines whether you qualify for loans and the interest rate you pay. Having excellent credit saves you tens of thousands on mortgages and other big purchases later in life.

Here are smart ways for millennials to build their credit score:

- Become an authorized user on someone else's old credit card. Their good payment history lifts your score too.

- Only open new credit cards when you need them to keep your utilization low. Applying for multiple cards short-term dings your score.

- Keep credit card balances below 30% of the limit. High balances relative to your limit hurts your score.

- Set up automatic payments to avoid ever missing a payment due to forgetfulness.

- Limit credit checks when shopping for a mortgage, auto loan, etc. Each check dings your score a few points. Do rate comparisons in a short period.

- Be cautious closing old credit cards as this lowers your total credit limit and increases utilization. Keep old accounts open.

- Build a long credit history by getting a credit card early on and responsibly keeping the account open.

- Pay off collections accounts and legal issues. If the adverse information is real, pay it and ask for it to be removed from your credit report.

Patience and diligently building good credit habits will boost your score over time. Having excellent credit accelerates your financial success by qualifying you for the best loan rates.

Chapter 3 Summary

- Pay off high interest "bad" debt aggressively using the debt snowball method

- Strategically utilize "good" debt like mortgages to generate greater wealth

- Make extra payments toward principal balances to pay off student loans faster

- Ask credit card companies to lower rates or consolidate debt onto a 0% balance transfer card

- Pay credit cards early and often to reduce interest payments

- Build long credit history and keep utilization low to improve credit score

Chapter 4: Building an Emergency Fund

Having quick access to cash in an emergency is crucial to avoiding debt. Your car breaks down. You get hit with medical bills. You lose your job.

Without savings, you are forced to rely on credit cards or payday loans when disaster strikes. But with an emergency fund, you can confidently handle life's curveballs.

In this chapter, you'll learn how to start building your rainy day fund. We'll cover how much you need to save and smart strategies to build your emergency savings faster.

How Much Emergency Savings Do You Need?

Aim to eventually save 3-6 months of living expenses in your emergency fund. This gives you a healthy buffer for most situations.

To determine how much that is, tally up your fixed monthly expenses:

- Rent / mortgage

- Minimum debt payments

- Insurance

- Utilities

- Food

- Transportation

- Medical costs

For a more conservative estimate, use your *take home pay* rather than expenses. This accounts for a total job loss where expenses need to be covered by savings.

If you earn $3,000 per month after taxes, aim to save $9,000 - $18,000 in emergency savings to cover 3 to 6 months.

Building up to the full 3-6 month target takes time. Start with $500 or $1000. Then add to it consistently each month. Even $25 per week adds up.

Once you've saved 1 month's worth, move onto investing extra money rather than just stockpiling too much cash. The key is finding the ideal emergency fund balance for your situation.

Having this safety net in savings eliminates the need to rely on credit cards or loans when faced with an emergency.

Where to Keep Your Emergency Money

Emergency fund money needs to be easily accessible when needed, but also earn a reasonable return while you save. Here's where to stash your savings:

High yield savings account – Compared to a traditional savings account, these pay up to 5X the interest while still allowing easy access to your money. Some top high yield savings accounts include CIT Bank, Marcus by Goldman Sachs, and Synchrony Bank.

Money market account – Very similar to high yield savings accounts. Money market accounts typically allow check writing and ATM access for quick emergency withdrawals when needed.

Short term CDs – Certificate of deposits pay slightly higher interest, but you can't access the money for the term of the CD without paying a penalty. Use CDs once you've already saved enough in an emergency fund account.

Online checking account – An online checking account with no minimum balance pays modest interest. Compared to brick-and-mortar banks, they have zero or low monthly fees.

Avoid investing your emergency fund in stocks or bonds which can lose value when you need the cash urgently. The online savings and checking accounts pay enough interest to keep your money working for you without much risk.

Resisting the Temptation to Raid Your Fund

Once an emergency fund is built up, fight the urge to tap it for non-essential expenses. Emergency funds are for *true* emergencies only:

- Sudden job loss

- Surprise medical bills

- Critical home or auto repairs

- Family emergency

If you lose discipline, your emergency savings will be drained by:

- Electronics upgrades

- Taking a vacation

- Making impulse purchases

- Paying routine bills

To avoid raiding your fund, pretend the money doesn't even exist. Automate regular contributions so you never see the full balance. Name the savings account something like "For Emergencies Only" as a reminder.

When you face a surprise expense, pause and ask yourself, "Is this truly a dire emergency that justifies dipping into my savings?" If not, find another solution like putting it on a 0% credit card and paying it off over time.

Never Tapping the Emergency Fund

What if you face an emergency but want to avoid tapping your savings at all costs? Here are alternatives to preserve your emergency fund:

- 0% credit cards: Transfer the balance when the introductory period ends

- Borrow from family or friends: Agree upon repayment terms

- Tax refund: The IRS offers loans against your expected refund

- Hardship withdrawal: 401k plans allow these for emergencies

- Low interest loan: Banks offer personal loans cheaper than credit cards

- Employer advance: Ask for your paycheck a few days early

- Payment plans: Work out installments directly with service providers

- Cut expenses: Reduce spending temporarily until you are past the crisis

Your #1 priority is avoiding high interest debt like payday loans or maxing out credit cards. But explore other options before depleting your emergency savings fund when possible.

In review, target saving 3-6 months of living expenses in your emergency fund. Store the money in easily accessible accounts like high yield savings and money market accounts. Only tap the funds for true financial emergencies. Your future self will thank you for having this security blanket!

Chapter 4 Summary

- Shoot for eventually saving 3-6 months of expenses in your emergency fund

- High yield savings accounts and money market funds are great places to stash emergency cash

- Start small if needed, saving just $25 per week

- Only use emergency savings for true emergencies, not routine expenses

- Explore alternatives like 0% credit cards before raiding your emergency fund

Chapter 5: Retirement Savings in Your 20s

Saving for retirement probably seems silly when you're just starting your career. Retirement is decades away!

But thanks to the power of compound interest, saving in your 20s sets you up for a comfortable retirement later in life. The decades give your money maximum time to grow.

In this chapter, you'll learn just how huge of an impact saving early makes. We'll cover the different retirement accounts to utilize and smart strategies to maximize your retirement contributions.

Taking Advantage of Compound Interest

Compound interest is when the interest earned gets added to your principal balance so that the next period's interest is calculated on the new, higher balance.

When repeated over decades, compounding can help your retirement savings grow exponentially. Compounding works fastest when you have more time.

Say you invest $10,000 and earn a 7% annual return. Here's how that compounds over different time periods:

- 5 years = $14,025

- 10 years = $19,671

- 20 years = $38,697

- 30 years = $76,122

An extra 10 years resulted in almost double the ending balance!

Now imagine starting retirement contributions in your 20s and letting compounding work its magic over 30-40 years by the time you retire.

Starting early and consistently investing allows compounding to transform seemingly small amounts into very large nest eggs given enough time.

The following table illustrates this by showing how much you would have at age 65 based on when you started saving:

Age Started Saving	Annual Contribution	Portfolio Value at 65
25	$3,000	$718,814
35	$3,000	$284,530
45	$3,000	$103,786

By starting just 10 years earlier - at 25 instead of 35 - you end up with over $400k more by retirement age!

That's because of the extra decade compounding had to grow your money. Waiting means you need to save a lot more per year to catch up. Take advantage of time and start saving early!

Types of Retirement Accounts

Where you save for retirement is just as important as when you start. Using tax-advantaged accounts boosts returns by reducing your tax bill.

Here are the best retirement accounts to utilize in your 20s:

401(k)s – Offered by your employer. Contributions come out of your paycheck pre-tax lowering your taxable income. Many employers also match a % of your contributions.

Roth IRAs – You contribute after-tax income but withdrawals in retirement are tax-free. Has income limits to qualify. In 2022, you can contribute up to $6,000 per year.

Traditional IRAs – Contributions are pre-tax but withdrawals in retirement are taxed as income. No income limits. 2022 contribution max is $6,000.

Health Savings Account (HSA) – Triple tax advantage. Contributions are pre-tax, growth is tax-free, and withdrawals for medical expenses are tax-free too. The 2022 contribution limit is $3650 for individuals.

Open a Roth IRA and contribute at least enough to max out any employer 401(k) match. Fund both consistently each month. Automate contributions so saving becomes effortless.

Setting Realistic Savings Goals

How much should you aim to save yearly for retirement? A good guideline is to save 10-15% of your gross income including any employer contributions.

If you earn $50,000 per year, aim to save $5,000 - $7,500 toward retirement annually. Break that down into monthly amounts like $400-$625.

Can you afford to save 15%? Start with 10% if needed and incrementally increase the percentage over time. The key is to start now, even if you can only afford small amounts.

Once your company 401(k) contributions max out the yearly limit ($20,500 in 2022 if you're under 50), open and fund an IRA with any additional savings.

Utilize 401(k) calculators to estimate your target monthly or yearly savings amount based on your current age, desired retirement age, income, and projected rate of return.

As you receive raises over your career, incrementally increase retirement contributions. Automate this so your lifestyle comfortably adjusts to the higher savings rate.

Employer Match Programs

If your employer offers a 401(k) match program, you absolutely want to contribute enough to claim the full match.

This is free money that boosts your retirement savings. A 50% match on 5% of your salary could add $2,500 per year to your 401(k).

Yet shockingly, 1 in 5 employees don't take advantage of the full 401(k) match their company offers. Don't leave this free retirement money on the table!

Before contributing to other accounts like an IRA, first make sure you're maxing out what your employer will match. Then use other accounts to reach your overall retirement savings goals.

Always opt for the Roth 401(k) version if offered. While you can't deduct Roth contributions like with a traditional 401(k), tax-free growth and withdrawals are more valuable long run.

Investment Basics

Within your retirement accounts you need to invest the money rather than just let it sit as cash. This is what enables compound growth through higher investment returns.

As a beginner, start by investing in target date index funds. These are a set-it-and-forget-it fund that automatically adjusts the asset allocation for you over time.

Target date funds are named by the approximate year you plan to retire. For example, a "Target 2060 Fund" diversifies your money across stocks and bonds appropriate for someone planning to retire around 2060.

Other good options are index funds that track major market indexes like the S&P 500. The average annual return of the S&P 500 is around 10% historically.

Steer clear of investing in individual stocks and speculative assets like cryptocurrencies in retirement accounts unless you really know what you're doing. Stick to broad index funds.

As you gain more investing experience over the years, you may branch out into other types of assets. But target date and index funds are great beginner set-it-and-forget-it options.

The key is to start investing those retirement contributions as early as possible. Over decades, compound growth will work wonders! Don't leave retirement accounts sitting in cash.

Chapter 5 Summary

- Start saving for retirement in your 20s to maximize compound growth

- Contribute enough to get any employer 401(k) match then fully fund a Roth IRA

- Save 10-15% of income toward retirement, increasing contributions over time

- Target date index funds are a hands-off way for beginners to invest retirement savings

- Take full advantage of tax benefits from 401(k)s, Roth IRAs, HSAs and other accounts

Here is a 1700 word draft for Chapter 6 on Smart Housing Decisions in markdown format:

Chapter 6: Smart Housing Decisions

Whether to rent or buy is often the biggest financial decision millennials face early in their career. Home ownership is part of the American dream. But it's also a complex financial move.

In this chapter, we'll explore rent vs buy considerations. You'll learn tips for saving for a down payment faster along with mortgage basics. We'll also cover common mistakes to avoid as a first-time homebuyer.

With smart strategic planning, you can time a home purchase to build equity and wealth using leverage responsibly.

Rent vs Buy Analysis

The rent vs buy decision depends on factors like:

Home prices in your area - In expensive markets, renting often wins financially unless staying long-term. Use the NY Times rent vs buy calculator to run scenarios.

Mobility - If moving frequently for new jobs, renting maintains flexibility. Buying has substantial transaction costs when selling.

Current savings - A 20% down payment helps avoid expensive PMI payments. Can you save 20% as a renter quickly?

Taxes - Mortgage interest and property taxes are deductible. Weigh lost deductions when renting.

Future plans - If you may relocate soon for a relationship, renting has advantages.

Maintenance costs - Owning means DIY repairs or paying for service costs. Calculate total costs.

Rent comparisons - Is renting cheaper per month than owning a similar property after insurance, taxes, etc?

Investment opportunities - The down payment money could also be invested instead. Compare potential returns.

Crunch the numbers for your situation. Buying isn't always the smarter financial move, especially for short duration stays.

Down Payment Tips and Programs

Ideally you want to make a 20% down payment when buying a home to avoid private mortgage insurance (PMI). PMI protects the lender, not you, and is an added monthly cost.

Here are tips for saving up for a robust down payment faster as a first-time buyer:

- **Save aggressively** - Make housing savings a top priority in your budget. Funnel windfalls like bonuses and tax refunds straight into your down payment fund.

- **Choose roommates** - Having roommates slashes housing costs, freeing up more money to save.

- **Invest lump sums** - Letting one-time infusions like inheritance or work bonuses compound via investing can grow your down payment faster long-term. Use retirement accounts to let them compound tax-free.

- **Delay purchases** - Postpone buying expensive items like luxury cars that will slow saving for the priority - a home down payment.

- **Negotiate salary increases** - Getting even a 5% bigger raise because you successfully negotiated means 5% more money that can go toward your goal each paycheck.

- **Take advantage of down payment assistance programs** - First-time buyer programs like HomeReady offer competitive interest rates and down payment assistance. FHA loans allow down payments as low as 3.5%.

Saving a 20% down payment while also having separate emergency savings plus closing costs takes disciplined budgeting. But the payoff of no PMI and instant equity is well worth the sacrifice.

Understanding Mortgages and Interest

Mortgages allow leveraging "other people's money" (the bank's) to purchase an asset like real estate. You gain control of a $500k house by only putting down $100k plus taking out a mortgage loan for the remaining $400k.

This leverage magnifies both gains and losses. You earn full returns on the $500k value while only contributing the $100k down payment. But if the home value drops, you take losses on the full amount as well.

This makes mortgages fundamentally different from buying a car or furniture via loan. A mortgage leverages you into an asset so you can build wealth. Other loans simply let you consume more than you otherwise could.

Mortgages accrue interest based on the type:

Fixed rate - Interest rate stays constant for the full term, normally 15 or 30 years. Predictable monthly payments.

ARM - Adjustable rate mortgage with fluctuating interest based on broader rate changes. Riskier.

Jumbo - For luxury homes above $647,200 in value. Require excellent credit and income.

FHA loan - Insured by the Federal Housing Administration. Just 3.5% down payment required.

Interest is owed on the principal loan balance each period. As you pay down principal over time, less interest accrues. This is the power of amortization.

Choose a fixed rate mortgage in a lower interest rate environment. ARMs become riskier when rates increase. Focus on interest rate, not just monthly payment.

Avoiding Common Homebuyer Mistakes

It's easy to get emotionally swept up in buying a home. But avoid these classic first-timer mistakes:

Overimproving - Don't gut renovate until you've lived in the home and understand how you use the space. Minor cosmetic fixes are fine initially.

House poor - Just because the bank approves you for a certain mortgage doesn't mean you should spend up to that limit. Build in a housing budget cushion.

No inspections - Pay for an independent home inspection to avoid buying hidden problems. Thoroughly check the roof, pipes, foundation.

No research - Understand average home pricing for the neighborhood. Overpaying sets you back on equity.

Impulse buying - Sleep on any purchase for at least a night to allow the emotions to dissipate and logic to return. Don't rush!

Fad renovations - Trends like open concept kitchens come and go. Stick to classic finishes for the best resale value.

DIY-ing important projects - Some home projects like electrical and plumbing need licensed professionals. Don't cut corners that could turn into safety hazards.

The key is thinking through the home buying decision rationally. Do your diligence on the property, neighborhood pricing, and financing terms. Patience lands you the best deal.

Chapter 6 Summary

- Compare rent vs buy scenarios in your area using online calculators

- Tips to save for a down payment faster like living with roommates

- Understand leverage - mortgages magnify gains and losses

- Opt for fixed rate mortgages over adjustable ARMs

- Research homes thoroughly and bring in inspectors before purchasing

- Don't fall into "house poor" situation or overimprove initially

Chapter 7: Side Hustles for Extra Cash

A side hustle provides the opportunity to boost your income and speed up financial goals. The extra money generated can pay off debt, bulk up savings, or be invested for the future faster.

But side hustling isn't for everyone. It takes time and effort outside of your regular job. In this chapter, we'll explore the pros and cons of side gig work. You'll get ideas for potential hustles both online and local. Tips are also provided on managing a side job without burning out.

Wield side hustles strategically to give your finances a surge when you need it most. They provide income flexibility and insulation against career disruptions.

Pros and Cons of Side Gig Work

Side hustling offers these financial benefits:

Increases total income – Bring home more money each month to improve cash flow for goals like debt repayment. Even an extra $500 can make a noticeable difference.

Allows you to build multiple income streams – One job loss won't wreck you financially. Income diversification creates stability.

Taps into different interests – Monetize your hobbies or develop new skills. Turn fun side pursuits into profitable gigs.

Provides way to test new careers – Try out a new field like real estate or copywriting without fully quitting your job yet.

Grows your network – Interacting with new clients and industries expands your connections. Great for career growth.

Creates a fallback option if you lose or quit your job – Having an established side business makes a job gap less financially stressful.

Opens the door for full-time entrepreneurship down the road – A successful side hustle can grow into a lucrative main hustle and business.

Improves retirement savings – Every extra dollar earned can be invested into retirement accounts like IRAs to compound over decades.

However, side hustles come with downsides to consider as well:

Require time and effort – Hours spent working side gigs reduce free time for family, relationships, and fun. Burnout is real.

Come with hassles of running a business - You must handle legalities, accounting, marketing, customer service, etc. These admin tasks add up fast.

Can negatively impact performance in your regular job – Juggling too many obligations hurts productivity and quality of work at your day job.

Additional tax paperwork – You'll likely need to file quarterly estimated payments on side income and track business deductions. More tax prep work results.

Limits unemployment benefits if you lose day job – Some states reduce benefits if you earned significant side income. Check local laws.

May necessitate lifestyle adjustment – Taking on clients or gigs every night and weekend will force changes to habits, routines and social life. Don't overcommit.

Think carefully before dive into side hustling. Understand the effort involved and how it will impact other areas of your life. Find the right life-work balance.

Turning Hobbies Into Income Streams

Monetizing activities and skills you already enjoy is the best way to side hustle without burning out. Explore these hobby areas:

Photography - Sell photos through stock sites like Shutterstock. Offer photography services for events, portraits, real estate listings. Teach classes on using cameras and editing tools.

Writing – Start a blog, publish an e-book, offer copywriting services, publish articles on Medium. Tons of opportunities to make money writing online or locally.

Crafts - Sell handmade crafts and artwork on Etsy, offer classes teaching your craft skills, create custom pieces on commission, set up a booth at local fairs.

Cooking - Bake and sell specialty cakes or treats, create meal plans and recipes to sell online, teach cooking classes in your home or at local restaurants.

Music - Offer private instrument lessons, record customized songs for occasions like birthdays and weddings, perform paid local gigs at wineries, fairs and restaurants.

Plants – Sell cuttings and plants you've propagated, create garden design plans for clients, maintain residential or commercial gardens.

Fitness – Become a virtual trainer and share workout videos online, teach paid outdoor bootcamp classes, lead a running group, train clients one-on-one.

What unique skills, knowledge and interests can you monetize? Identify your personal passions first, then brainstorm potential ways to generate cash from them.

Creating an Online Business or Selling Products

You don't have to limit side hustling to local clients. The internet allows you to sell products and services that scale worldwide 24/7.

With platforms like Shopify, Etsy, Amazon Handmade, and eBay, selling online is easier than ever:

- **Sell digital products** – Create design templates, photo filters, courses, e-books, stock media. No inventory required.

- **Dropship goods** – Find suppliers to ship products directly to customers so you don't handle fulfillment and inventory.

- **Sell print-on-demand products** – Upload your art and designs to be printed on shirts, mugs, hats when customers order them. The company handles printing and shipping.

- **Start an ecommerce store** – Create your own online storefront to sell physical products you source and fulfill yourself. Requires more effort but higher profit margins.

You can even build entire businesses around your skills and knowledge by going digital:

- Offer consulting services relevant to your career expertise

- Build an agency focusing on social media management, web design, video production

- Launch an online tutoring service teaching academic subjects or specialized skills

- Create online courses teaching others your expertise through recorded video lessons

The internet provides unlimited possibilities for monetizing your natural abilities from anywhere.

Managing a Side Hustle Alongside a Regular Job

Juggling side work alongside a full-time job demands discipline and organization. Here are tips to make it sustainable long-term:

- **Set firm boundaries** – Limit side gig hours to nights and weekends. Protect your downtime. Communicate availability clearly to prevent burnout.

- **Designate business hours** – Running a social media consulting agency? Only respond to clients during stated hours, not 24/7.

- **Block time rigorously** – Use a calendar to block out both your day job and side hustle commitments. This ensures everything gets done without overwhelm.

- **Outsource tasks** – Pay for a virtual assistant to handle customer service, order fulfillment, social media, or other tasks that take up your precious time. This liberates you to focus on the higher value work only you can do in your business.

- **Automate where possible** – Use tools like Calendly for automated appointment booking rather than exchanging countless emails. Apps like Buffer can schedule social media content in advance.

- **Take breaks** - Build in dedicated days each week for recharging and spending time with family or friends. Don't hustle nonstop.

- **Keep finances separate** - Open a dedicated side hustle checking account and credit card. This simplifies bookkeeping and protects any legal liability.

The right systems and boundaries enable a fulfilling side hustle without burning out. Your health, relationships and performance at your day job should never suffer.

Chapter 7 Summary

- Side hustles allow you to earn extra money while exploring new skills and interests

- Monetize existing hobbies to make profitable side gigs more enjoyable

- Sell digital and physical products online 24/7 through platforms like Shopify and Etsy

- Use automation and outsourcing so a side business doesn't consume all your bandwidth

- Set firm work hours and calendar blocks to prevent side hustle burnout

Conclusion

Congratulations, you've made it to the end of Money Mastery for Millennials! By reading this book, you've taken a huge step toward getting your finances in order as a young adult.

This final chapter recaps the key lessons and strategies covered throughout the book. I'll provide final thoughts on maintaining the money mindset, habits and skills needed to thrive financially in your 20s and beyond.

Key Takeaways

Here are the core principles to remember:

Master the foundations - Budgeting, managing debt, building an emergency fund, and starting retirement savings now provide the basis for a secure financial future.

Change money mindsets - Adopt empowering beliefs about money through daily affirmations. Visualize and feel what future financial success will bring.

Save aggressively - Make saving a priority. Pay yourself first each paycheck and automate transfers into investment accounts. Time in the market is more powerful than timing the market.

Educate yourself - Read personal finance books, listen to podcasts, follow money mentors on social media. Knowledge conquers fear and puts you firmly in control of your finances.

Invest early and often - Harness the incredible power of compound interest by starting to invest in your 20s. Contribute consistently and reinvest all gains.

Build alternative income streams - Whether through side hustles, real estate or other investments, diversify your income sources. Multiple streams provide stability if you lose your primary job.

Make money decisions rationally - Don't act on emotions. Sleep on big purchases. Seek wise counsel from mentors. Crunch the numbers.

Delay gratification today for a better tomorrow - Small lifestyle sacrifices allow outsized investment in your future self through saving and investing.

You are the average of the people you spend time with - If your friends are all broke, it's easy to remain stuck in bad money habits together. Seek out friends and mentors who uplift and inspire you financially. Their mindsets will rub off.

Adopting even a few of these principles consistently will propel you leagues ahead of peers financially. Small daily choices compound into enormous results over decades.

Maintaining Good Money Habits

Transforming your financial life doesn't require depriving yourself or making huge sacrifices. It's more about building tiny money habits that, over time, produce amazing results.

Here are a few habits to practice daily:

- Pay yourself first by automating savings and investment transfers

- Check your spending account balance daily and celebrate steady progress

- Cook meals at home and pack lunch rather than ordering takeout

- Brew coffee instead of stopping at Starbucks

- Walk, bike or take public transit to avoid gas and parking costs

- Pursue free activities like local hikes or museum visits

- Create goals for each savings category and track progress

- Review monthly budgets and spending before the new month starts

- Read personal finance books or blogs during your commute

- Unplug from email for chunks of time to improve productivity

These micro-habits take little effort but move your finances inches forward every single day.

You Are in Control of Your Financial Future

Remember that you alone get to shape your financial life. It comes down to the small repeated choices you make each day.

Don't believe the incorrect notion that only the rich can build wealth or that you have to deprive yourself to get ahead financially. With the right money mindset, habits and education, anyone can achieve financial success.

Be patient with yourself. Building wealth and breaking old money habits doesn't happen overnight. But month after month and year after year, incremental progress compounds.

I hope this book provided you the knowledge, mindsets and habits to empower yourself financially as a young adult.

Wishing you a lifetime of financial prosperity and security. You've got this!

Conclusion Summary

- Employ daily micro-habits that move your finances inches forward

- Knowledge, persistence and mindset are key - anyone can build wealth

- Be patient with yourself - financial success takes time but compounding works

- You are fully in control of your money future based on your daily choices

About the Author

A background in Economics and Business Administration equips Esther Bukar with a unique blend of academic knowledge and practical experience. She passionately advocates for financial literacy and empowerment, dedicating herself to assisting millennials in achieving their financial goals by taking control over their finances.

Esther cultivated a profound comprehension of economic principles and financial management strategies during her academic journey. Early on, she acknowledged the significance of financial education; thus, she endeavored to impart her wisdom—especially to young adults grappling with the intricate web that is personal finance.

Esther, propelled by her fervent aspiration to influence significantly, undertook the mission of demystifying money management and instilling in millennials an ability to construct a robust financial base. She compiled "Money Mastery for Millennials: The No-Nonsense Guide to Managing Your Money in Your 20s" drawing from personal experiences and extensive research; this resource offers pragmatic advice - customised for young adults' distinctive needs and challenges.

Esther engages actively in financial education initiatives within her community, alongside her writing. She orchestrates workshops: seminars--and even webinars; these cover an array of topics including budgeting, saving, investing and debt management. Her efforts reach individuals from diverse backgrounds – empowering them to take control of their own financial futures.

Believing in everyone's entitlement to financial freedom and security, Esther harbors a profound commitment towards financial education. Her work aspires not only to inspire but also empower millennials: she wants them taking control of their finances--making informed decisions that pave the way for living life on their own terms.

Esther, not one to be deeply engrossed in the realm of personal finance at all times; she indulges her other interests – traveling; delving into new cuisines; and cherishing moments with loved ones. She advocates for a balanced lifestyle—urging individuals to chase their passions while simultaneously prioritizing their health.

Esther Bukar, the author of "Money Mastery for Millennials," passionately equips young adults with knowledge in finance, instilling confidence and sharpening skills necessary to master their finances; she propels them towards a brighter future--financially speaking.